DUST TO DUST

DUST TO DUST

by Robert Farquhar

JOSEF WEINBERGER PLAYS

LONDON

DUST TO DUST
First published in 2002
by Josef Weinberger Ltd
12-14 Mortimer Street, London, W1T 3JJ

Copyright © 2002 by Robert Farquhar

The author has asserted his moral right to be identified as the author of this work in accordance with sections 77 and 78 of the Copyright Designs and Patents Act 1988.

ISBN 0 85676 270 9

This play is protected by Copyright. According to Copyright Law, no public performance or reading of a protected play or part of that play may be given without prior authorisation from Josef Weinberger Plays, as agent for the Copyright Owners.

From time to time it is necessary to restrict or even withdraw the rights of certain plays. **It is therefore essential to check with us before making a commitment to produce a play.**

NO PERFORMANCE MAY BE GIVEN WITHOUT A LICENCE

AMATEUR PRODUCTIONS
Royalties are due at least one calendar month prior to the first performance. A royalty quotation will be issued upon receipt of the following details:

Name of Licensee
Play Title
Place of Performance
Dates and Number of Performances
Audience Capacity
Ticket Prices

PROFESSIONAL PRODUCTIONS
All enquiries regarding professional rights should be addressed to Brie Burkeman, 14 Neville Court, Abbey Road, London NW8 9DD.

OVERSEAS PRODUCTIONS
Applications for productions overseas should be addressed to our local authorised agents. Further details are listed in our catalogue of plays, published every two years, or available from Josef Weinberger Plays at the address above.

CONDITIONS OF SALE
This book is sold subject to the condition that it shall not by way of trade or otherwise be resold, hired out, circulated or distributed without prior consent of the Publisher. **Reproduction of the text either in whole or part and by any means is strictly forbidden.**

Printed by Watkiss Studios Ltd, Biggleswade, Beds, England

For Sue without whom I would have given up, and
in memory of Tom Farquhar (1918-1996).

Thanks to John Chatterton for driving me
to the edge of Britain.

DUST TO DUST was first performed at the Unity Theatre, Liverpool on January 15th 2001 by Peccadillo Theatre Company, with the following cast:

HENRY	Ron Meadows
HOLLY	Jane Hogarth
KEV	Warren Donnelly

Directed by Sarah Thornton

DUST TO DUST was subsequently presented at the Assembly Rooms, Edinburgh as part of the 2002 Edinburgh Fringe Festival on August 2nd 2002. The play was produced by Richard Jordan Productions Ltd in association with Peccadillo Theatre Company with the following cast:

HENRY	Ron Meadows
HOLLY	Julie Riley
KEV	Warren Donnelly

Directed by Sarah Thornton

A bare stage. In the darkness, music. 'Angel of Death' by Hank Williams. The lights rise. All three characters enter, firstly KEV, *then* HOLLY, *and finally* HENRY.

HENRY　　OK.
It was the middle of the night.
I was asleep
As you tend to be
And the phone rang.
And immediately you think, fuck, what's going on?
A phone call, this time of night?
I mean, it's not going to be someone ringing you up to tell you you've won the lottery
And the phone was under the bed for some reason.
And you know it's there somewhere but it's just not quite
You can't find the fucking thing
And it keeps on ringing
Ring bloody ring
It just keeps on bloody ringing
And I remember thinking
Well there's that bit of you that thinks it's going to be something terrible
But then more often than not
It'll be a wrong number
Someone arsing about
And eventually, after upending an ashtray, and there's bloody dog-ends falling about all over the place, I find it
And there was a voice at the other end.
Not unsurprisingly
And this voice seems to know my name.
And this voice, this, policeman, as it turns out
This policeman asks me if I know a Michael Finnegan.

HOLLY　　I remember I was late for work that day.
I'd blame the alarm clock, but I haven't got one
Anyway I made it to the Institute with a minute to spare.

All the usual culprits present and correct
Mostly old people
And Precious, 'teacher', she was there,
sharpening her pencils, and cracking jokes with
the pensioners about their sex lives
And I nipped behind the screen, whipped my
clothes off, and put on the dressing-gown.
It's a big heavy paisley thing.
Apparently it makes me look very Pre-Raphaelity.
Anyway I did the class.
Mostly sitting, and a couple of things with a scarf.
It's not a bad way to earn a living.
Not that I earn a living but you know what I mean.
And people often ask me
Because it's one of those jobs that people always
have questions about
And they often ask me what do I think about
You know when I'm standing there or sitting there
or whatever I'm doing
Anyway it made me realise that I do tend to drift
off
So now
And I'll warn you this is a bit wanky
Now I try to do a sort of meditation
A memory meditation
As it's called
I got the idea from a book
I try to recall moments, memories
And then I try to remember other memories from
that time or that I associate with that particular
memory
And you have to be very specific
That's the key apparently
I said it was a bit wanky
But that's what I try to do
Often I do drift off
But that's the plan
And that day
And I'm not making this up
I recalled the time we went to Scotland
Camping
Me and Mick
In his godawful beige tent with the brown
groundsheet

And his motorbike
And the sunglasses he bought me
And the dog in the car with the lampshade on its
head
It wasn't a real lampshade it was one of those
things dogs wear to stop them scratching
themselves
But I hadn't thought about that moment since
Christ knows when
And actually I laughed slightly when I was
thinking about it
And one of the old dears said 'penny for your
thoughts'
Bless her
And I thought about those few days
I thought about other stuff too
The row in the service station
But
It seems a bit spooky maybe
But I did think of that time
Scotland
Och aye, bonnie Scotland
And Mick going on about going to live up there
In a cottage that we'd do up apparently
He was always full of it
And this from someone who thought a spirit level
was something you used when measuring whiskey
And the class finished and we went for a coffee
And we were chatting
Precious was telling me I should try acupuncture
for my insomnia
And I said that sounds a bit painful
But then I noticed my sister
Carmel
She was obviously looking for me
And she came over
And she stood there and she said had I heard
And I laughed at the way she said it
But then she said she'd better sit down
And I realised this wasn't just a bit of gossip
And Precious said should she go?
And I said no stay
So Carmel sat down and she told me

KEV I heard that Mick was dead from some fellar called Darren.
He's just some bloke from the pub.
I don't really know him, but somehow he'd heard
So when he tapped me on the shoulder
I was getting myself a Twix
From a kiosk
And I turned round and there he was
Whats-his-face
Darren
I was slightly taken aback
He seemed
For a start he was smiling
And he said have you heard about Mick?
And I said Mick? Mick Finnegan?
And he said yea, he's dead, apparently he fell down some stairs.
And when he was saying this, he was still smiling
So I said, are you joking
And he laughed and he said no what sort of sick fucker did I think he was
And then someone shouted him from across the road and he belted off
And that was it
That was how I heard Mick was dead
I'd only been chatting with him the night before
And now apparently he was dead
I remember thinking
That it was all a bit
Odd
So
I had a wander
I didn't eat the Twix
I gave it to some fellar selling The Big Issue
And I went to the meat market
I was thinking of my tea
But the smell got to me
So I headed back to the office
But just outside I stepped in some dog stuff
I wasn't really looking where I was going
I tried to clean it off in the toilets
Quite a difficult operation as I had my black shoes on with the fancy soles so it was sort of
You know

Dust to Dust

                In between the crevices
                Anyway I managed
                Although the smell was still noticeable
                And I sat at my desk
                And
                Everyone was doing what they normally did
                I tried to do some work
                But I didn't feel right
                I pleaded a fuzzy head, Spanish flu
                There's been a spate recently
                I don't know why it's Spanish
                And I took the afternoon off
                Nobody seemed to mind
                And I got a taxi
                Five pounds sixty
                And I went to The Bulls Head.

HENRY   They phoned me because apparently Mick's
                downstairs neighbour, the bloke who actually
                found him, lying there at the bottom of the stairs,
                when the police asked him who Mick's next of kin
                was, the best he could come up with was me.
                Which is probably true to some extent.
                He has got a brother in Cornwall.
                They are, were, not the closest, let's say.
                But still, I phoned him.
                I've got some bad news, I said.
                I mean, good line, a tad cliche yes, but make the
                most of it is what I say, if you know what I mean
                But in the dramatic pause he says, Mick's dead
                isn't he
                Before I could tell him
                He pre-empts
                And I said yea, yea he is, he fell down some stairs,
                pissed probably
                And even before I'd finished saying it I wish I
                hadn't said it
                Those last two words
                Pissed probably
                Not
                It's true but
                Not that Mick would have given a shit
                And he goes quiet
                Silent

I've met him once and he never said much then but this, this is slightly unnerving
He said he'd come to the funeral, but he didn't want to have anything to do with the organising
Anyway he goes silent
And I think he's maybe crying
Holding it back
You know that way sometimes
You see people do it in documentaries
But eventually he says
I'm not surprised
I'm not surprised?
Not oh dear I am a bit upset
Not well that's ruined my fucking weekend then
No
I'm not surprised.
And do you know what, I know what he meant.

HOLLY   And after Carmel tells me
They both look at me as though
As though something might happen
And Precious rubs me on the arm
I do feel shocked
One of the first things I thought was someone I've had sex with is dead
I didn't say it
But I thought it
And Carmel says what she's heard
She'd been told by her local newsagent can you believe
And then she says
She says
I always thought something like this might happen to Mick
Pause
What do you mean? I say
I always thought, you know, she says
No, I don't you know, I say
You know, I always thought he, could
And I say, what
And she pulls that face
That face that says oh come on he might have been your ex-husband but we all know he was a feckless fucking drifter when it comes down to it

Dust to Dust

It's quite a face
So I say it again
What? You always thought he could do what?
And Precious carries on rubbing my arm
There's the beginning of an atmosphere
Carmel's biting her lip
And I'm staring at the wall
There's an exhibition of pictures from Afghanistan
or somewhere
But eventually she says
Look, he was always a bit
And I can feel her thinking how shall I put this
He was always a bit on the edge
On the edge?
Oh Jesus the, the meaning, the, the sub-text, the
And what does that mean, I say
And she doesn't say anything
She just looks at Precious and they share a little
conspiratorial smile
What do you mean, I say
Slightly louder this time
And a few heads turn our way
Oh forget it, she says
And she shakes her head in that way
That way that says there's no talking to her in this
mood
That way that has always got right up my nose
And I go off
No other way to describe it
I start having a go
And Carmel starts having a go
Like two sisters who have always resented each
other's lifestyles tend to
And it's all the usual shit
All about the way I've lived my life
All about the men I choose to go with
Her words
And Precious is in the middle of this
She's a bit out of her depth
And eventually
Something has to give
And she storms off
She's very good at storming off is Carmel

Her final words being something along the lines of
'fuck off and die'
My family
Don't ask
And Precious takes me outside
And I bawl my head off
People walk past trying not to look
And she goes, go on let it all out
And I let it all out
And we sit there
We're on some steps
And a few minutes pass without us saying
anything
And eventually Precious says she has to go and
pick up her daughter
And she goes
And I stay sitting there on the steps
With everyone walking round me

KEV The Bulls Head was quiet
The shopping channel was on for some reason
There was a group of lads taking the piss out of it
And there were two young girls behind the bar
I asked them about Mick but neither of them was
entirely sure who he was
Although they said people had been in earlier
talking about it
So I had a pint
There was a *Daily Mirror* lying about
And I read about Catherine Zeta-Jones' yacht
How much her wallpaper cost
Four thousand pounds a roll apparently
And I was thinking maybe I should get off
But then
Henry came in
He was on his own
He looked
A bit lost in himself
And I was wondering should I leave him
But eventually I did sidle over
He didn't register me at first
I'm not normally in the pub this early
And after a bit
I said

I wasn't entirely sure how to start
I said
I'd heard about Mick
And he said
Yea, he'd heard about Mick too, he'd even seen him
And for a moment I thought I've got it all wrong, he's not
But then it turned out that he'd had been to identify the body
The police had phoned him up in the early hours apparently
Apparently he looked OK
I mean, you know
Considering he was dead
He just had a small cut above his left eye
They think it was a brain haemorrhage
And he said he was organising the funeral
And he was intending to get up to Mick's flat tomorrow
See what was what etcetera
And I said if he needed a hand I'd only be too willing
Because Mick, I said
I was
I was very fond of Mick
And he said, yea if I wanted
But we didn't mention it again as Brian and Davy Crockett turned up
And they got a round in
They even included me
And they wanted to hear Henry's story
And then a few others turned up
Chris and Max and that fellar who had his driving licence taken off him
You could tell everyone was a bit shocked
But you could also tell something was different
Everyone was drinking a bit faster

(*We start to hear* HENRY'S *speech underneath.*)

It was strange
Mick was dead
He'd been here only last night

And it was like it was Christmas or something
Not Christmas
But
But people were talking
It was different
And I bought a round
Fifteen pounds
Something like that
Everyone was talking about Mick
Everyone had a story
He was the sort of fellar everyone had a story about
It was getting quite noisy actually
And then I noticed
There was a change
People weren't talking so loud
And then Henry said

HENRY (*underneath* KEV) Hey hey
Do you remember the absinthe?
I don't know where do you get it from?
Mexico? I haven't got a clue
Three quid a shot that's right
Well he got a bottle somehow
Mail order I think I never asked
And oh my Christ
I was seeing treble
Quadruple
Literally I am not joking
And Mick got hold of that bike and was riding it round the bar of that strange pub
Oh wasn't he! Miserable sod
That was your bike?
I don't know mate
Maybe he'll give it back in his will
I shouldn't think so
What Mick?
I think there's more chance of me getting the next round in

HENRY But hey fuck it you only die once
Do you want another drink?

(HENRY *turns round.*)

HENRY	Holly
KEV	And there she was
HOLLY	They were all laughing Unbelievable Mick was dead And they were all laughing
HENRY	Holly? What I wanted to say what are you doing here? But in the circumstances it seemed a touch obvious.
KEV	She was wet through
HENRY	Let's put it like this I've seen her looking better
HOLLY	Oh The Bulls Head It was the sort of the place they refurbish every few years but within a week it always looks the same And they were all there The same old losers club The same old sad bastards And you could tell I'd made an impression And the saddest bastard of them all Then said He said Wait for this He said
HENRY	Do you want a drink?
HOLLY	That's what he said
KEV	And she was just standing there She was staring at Henry Looking straight at him
HENRY	Mick always said she had a scary stare

HOLLY	And And now I was there Now I was there I'd been drinking all afternoon I didn't know what to do
HENRY	And I thought fuck me I'm in a soap opera
KEV	And you could feel everyone slightly backing off
HOLLY	So having a good time are we? Having a drink for good old Mick then?
HENRY	And I thought good God she's even talking as though it's a soap opera Look do you want a drink?
HOLLY	I don't want a drink
HENRY	Come on
HOLLY	No
HENRY	Come on have a drink
HOLLY	I don't want a drink
HENRY	Have a drink!
HOLLY	No.
KEV	And then she leaves Out the door
HENRY	And someone I think it was Max He says 'you'd better go after her'
KEV	It was me actually
HENRY	And if there's one thing And Mick would agree with me on this If there's one thing you should always do when a woman storms off like that

	The one thing you always do is finish your drink
HOLLY	And it was still chucking it down
And I thought
Actually I was so drunk I wasn't thinking anything remotely coherent
All I wanted to do was go home, fall unconscious and start my life again
KEV	And Henry finishes his drink and heads for the door
And as he's about to exit he turns and says
HENRY	If I'm not back in three days send out the St Bernard
KEV	And we all laugh
HENRY	And there she was I can see the bloody drama queen hobbling about in a puddle off in the distance
HOLLY	And I'm getting wetter
There are no taxis anywhere
And everything is running through my head
And then I decide
I just decide
I am very pissed remember
I decide I'm going to go back
HENRY	And I go towards her
But this woman I think was Holly
It isn't
And she tells me to be gone from her life forthwith
HOLLY	And I turn back
HENRY	Roughly translatable as fuck off
KEV	And it must be two three minutes after Henry's left
And the door opens again and in walks
HOLLY	And I can tell they're surprised

KEV	She's even wetter than before
HOLLY	And Henry's not there now And one of them says I can't remember which one He says
KEV	I said he'd gone off looking for her
HOLLY	Oh that's good of him, I think.
KEV	And she still doesn't say anything
HOLLY	And I think fuck this
KEV	And she's out the door again
HOLLY	Fuck the lot of them
KEV	And someone says This was Max He says Maybe the brewery could get revolving doors put in And everyone laughs
HENRY	And I turn back I'm soaked through now And there she is She's coming out of The Bulls Head
KEV	And whilst everyone's still laughing I slip out
HOLLY	And there's Henry coming towards me
HENRY	And I start running down the road towards her And me and running we have never been the best of mates
HOLLY	And then as if out of nowhere
KEV	Holly hails a taxi

HOLLY	It does one of those mad U-turns
KEV	I got a bit splashed
HENRY	And she starts getting into a taxi And I think I am not having this
HOLLY	And I think, taxi driver, please take me home
HENRY	I've risked pneumonia and extreme social embarrassment For a woman who has always hated me unconditionally And I am fucked if I am having this
KEV	And Henry tries to pull her back out on to the pavement
HOLLY	And I'm holding onto the door because I want to go home
HENRY	It was not a dignified sight
KEV	And the taxi driver, he's losing his patience And tells them to finish their domestic on the pavement
HOLLY	Domestic? Domestic? Who did he think I was?
KEV	And he obviously wasn't joking as the next thing he's round the back of the cab and yanking Holly out
HOLLY	And he's a bit fucking rough actually
HENRY	Obviously I would have intervened but there are two sorts of people I never have physical altercations with
HOLLY	And I'm back on the pavement
HENRY	People who look like Mike Tyson and taxi drivers

KEV	And it's still raining
HOLLY	Although by this stage I am so wet I've given up caring
KEV	And the taxi drives off
HENRY	And she starts doing what Mick said she always did best Shouting About how I've always hated her How I should have phoned her Rather than her sister telling her Because the newsagent told her or something I don't know what she's going on about And I think this is fucking ridiculous because The last I'd heard she was in London
HOLLY	And that is such rubbish because I've been back from London over a year now
HENRY	Well how was I to know that I'm not her social secretary am I? And then she comes out with
HOLLY	I didn't mean it but basically I said he was responsible for Mick's death
HENRY	And, not unreasonably, I ask for further elaboration
HOLLY	And I said I said that Mick would never have drunk half as much as he did if it hadn't been for Henry
HENRY	And if you'd known Mick Which obviously might prove a tad difficult now You'd know that was total and utter bollocks
HOLLY	And then I said
HENRY	Just to clear up any grey areas

HOLLY	I said that Henry had killed him
	(*Silence.*)
HENRY	And there's not a lot you can say to that
HOLLY	I said it It's true to some extent I know I know, Mick never did anything he didn't want to do But if Henry hadn't been around I'm sure half the time he wouldn't have Oh don't listen to me
HENRY	She said I'd killed him She said that I She Fuck me Me? I'd What? Me?! And I am fucking livid
KEV	He was none too pleased
HOLLY	And although I know I shouldn't have said it I am quite pleased that I've upset him so much
KEV	And they're yelling at each other Far more than before
HENRY	I was ranting
HOLLY	And he starts on about me and Mick
HENRY	Only natural in the circumstances
HOLLY	About how our marriage was a sham How he's amazed that Mick didn't leave me earlier
HENRY	I know she left him but arguments like this Well, truth goes out the window doesn't it?

HOLLY	And then something about how if he'd been married to me he'd have been on heroin by now
HENRY	Always go for the jugular If there's nothing else two marriages has taught me At moments like this always do that
HOLLY	And I cut him off by saying if I'd been married to him I would have killed myself by now
HENRY	Which is bollocks because I know she always fancied me
KEV	The whole thing is not a pretty sight
HOLLY	And I'm out of control I'm wet I'm pissed I'm Everything had stopped being real
HENRY	And I think fuck this for a game of soldiers
HOLLY	Everything had stopped being real quite some time back
KEV	And Henry turns and heads off down the road
HENRY	I am sick of the whole bloody thing
HOLLY	And he goes
HENRY	Enough psychotic ex-wives for one evening thank you very much
HOLLY	And I carry on shouting after him
KEV	But then she stops Suddenly And she stands there And she starts Crying But more than crying

It's more
I've never seen anyone like it
Her whole body was rocking backwards and forwards
And I think
Shall I do something?
But
What?
And then she stops again
As suddenly as she started
She just stands there
And then there's another taxi

HOLLY   I'm not at all clear on this bit
But
There was someone talking to me
Sort of pushing me

KEV   She didn't seem to be making anything out

HOLLY   And
I was in the back of a cab

KEV   And she falls on the floor
I can see her knickers

HOLLY   Someone was asking me something

KEV   I didn't know where she lived
And the taxi driver he started looking a bit
I didn't want a scene like last time
And I think
Oh Christ I'd better go with her
And she muttered something
She had stuff running all down her nose
Anyway the taxi driver seemed to make sense of it
And we set off

HOLLY   And then we're in my street

KEV   And I think I'd better head back to mine
Work and all that
But she insists I get out with her
She won't let go of my hand

HOLLY	To be honest by this point I had no idea what I was doing
KEV	And I have to pay the fare Seven pounds including a tip
HOLLY	And there was my door Just over there But I couldn't seem to
KEV	I recognise vaguely where we are And Holly is babbling I can't make out what she's saying And she presses herself up against me She reeks of booze but she's still got that woman smell And I help her get her key out And she keeps trying to say something I don't think she really knows who I am And she looks at me And she says It's slurred but it still makes sense I loved him I loved him She keeps repeating it I loved him And she looks at me As though I might understand And It's quite awkward to be honest I was fond of Mick But obviously I didn't I mean He was just a bloke down the pub
HOLLY	And then I fell over
KEV	She just seemed to give way
HOLLY	Always my drunken party-piece
KEV	And I try and help her back on to her feet

HOLLY	And then Fuck me there's some dirty old git
KEV	I was just trying to help her up
HOLLY	There's some dirty old no-mark trying to feel me up And at moments like that
KEV	She obviously misread what I was trying to do
HOLLY	Your instincts kick in
KEV	I try and stay vertical but gravity is not having it And I topple backwards Sort of flapping my arms as I go
HOLLY	And I'm up the steps and through the door
KEV	And before I know it I'm on my backside And the door slams And I can hear her knocking something over in the corridor
HOLLY	Bollocks
KEV	And I think Shall I ring the bell See if she's alright (*Beat.*) But then I think she'll probably call the police if I do that (KEV *exits.*)
HOLLY	There were some messages on the machine Carmel Some pathetic attempt at an apology And next to the answer machine there's a mirror And I saw myself Not good Not good at all

                And I lean forward
                In the way that only very drunk people can
                I'm trying to look at myself
                I'm trying to figure out something
                Something to do with something
                Me
                Something to do with me
                And I keep leaning forward
                And I've got my face right up against the glass
                I can see all my pores
                The blotches
                The wrinkles
                And I think is this me
                Is this
                Is this what I look like

                (HENRY *enters.*)

HOLLY   Oh dear
                Not good
                Not good at all, Holly

HENRY   In fact looking shit, Henry
                That's what I was thinking
                I was standing at this bar
                There were mirrors all over the place
                Some modern architecty attempt at cutting-edge ambience
                Or some such bollocks
                And I thought you look dishevelled man
                You look as though you've seen the dead body of your best mate
                You look
                She thinks I killed Mick
                Mick
                I killed him?
                Fucking cheek
                She has got a fucking cheek
                Cheeky fucking
                Bimbo
                And this music
                Thump thump fucking thump
                Christ knows how I ended up there
                And it's full of trendy wankers

Students
Youth
Full of themselves
Full of their fucking lives in front of them
And their mobile phones ringing every fifteen seconds
Thump thump fucking thump
Call this fucking music
And I'm thinking of Mick
Stupid bastard
Laid out like he's getting a suntan
And then there's one group who come in
Mostly lads
Thinking their God's gift to something
One of them is even wearing dark glasses
And also I notice another one
He's wearing a t-shirt
And on it it says
'If you don't like my attitude fuck off'
That's what it says
Bold as bleeding brass
And I think
I am fucked if I'm going to fuck off just because his fucking t-shirt fucking tells me to
And I go over and I tell him this
And they think I'm joking
Having a laugh
But I'm not
Oh no I am deadly serious
I am making a point
Something about values society boundaries being crossed
All that
And then one of them does a fake yawn
And then mister t-shirt
He turns his back on me
He's had enough of me apparently
And so I sort of
I suppose I give him what can be best described as a push
And this push becomes a scuffle
And this scuffle becomes an altercation
And then
Starting fights has never been my forte

But somehow I do not seem to be doing too bad
And then
I hit him
Smack
Side of the face
And he tries to hit me back
And then I do something else
To the uninvolved onlooker it probably looked like some
Bizarre arty-ballet thing
And then someone tries to kick me
And I try and kick back
It's sort of Bruce Lee meets Norman Wisdom
A few people are shouting
'Get the lanky bastard'
That sort of thing
And then the bouncers are there
They've got my arm up the middle of my back
They're remarkably professional for bouncers in retrospect
But I'm still mad
And they try to escort me off the premises
But I am a wild mad bastard
I want to walk out of there with some dignity
And I struggle free
But
There's a small flight of stairs
And gravity being what it is
I do a nice little tumble
Through the air
Infact no other way to describe it
I am falling through the atmosphere

HOLLY   My face is pressed up against the mirror
And I keep looking
I keep looking in the vain pissed hope that
something will reveal itself
And I think of a time
A time from sometime back
And I think of booze
And I think of wine and beer and vodka and sweet cider sometimes
And how it'll be the death of us
I hate it

The smell of it
The after-taste of it
It's a poisonous bastard that shrinks your head
and makes you look like a gargoyle
And oh Mick loved his drink
He lusted it
He swam in it
'It was what kept us together
And it was what broke us apart'
And I think of that flat where we did all that drinking
And all that arguing
All that bittersweet bickering that went on and on for days and days
And I think of that time
And an argument
A piss poor attempt at a row that got out of hand
I can't even remember what is what about
Something to do with money
It always was
Something to do with the threadbare state of our lives
And we'd gone from sniping to backbiting to growling to full-blooded open warfare
You bitch you wanker you this you that
Non-fucking stop
Sometimes I think I've spent my whole life arguing
My whole life and it's not funny
And then he says, he says, I never wanted a wife
And I say, well it's a bit fucking late for that now
We're a bit too far down the cul-de-sac of life for you to be coming out with that shit
And he puts on a record
Hendrix
Loud
Scratched
It was that one with all the naked women on the front
The room is literally shaking
In other times this would be glorious
But this is bad
This smells rotten
This reeks of bad times gone worse
And I yank the needle off

	And the silence
	The silence is
	Very loud if you know what I mean
	And we look at each other
	What next eh?
	We're both thinking it
	You can almost hear our breathing
	And Mick
	He's not
	He doesn't look sane
	And he runs his fingers through his hair
	And he's wild
	Wilder than ever before
	And then he swings at something
	Not at me
	Something deeper
	Himself
	It's as though he's fucked with everything
	And he lashes out
	And there's a mirror
	Some cheapo tat from one of those cheapo tat shops that come and go
	And it cracks
	His elbow smacks into it
	It cracks down the middle and from the sides
	It implodes
	It falls
	It
	It gives up the will
	And it flops on the front room carpet
	A pathetic metaphor
	A cheapo useless piece of tat that I never should have bought in the first place
HENRY	And the table that I crash into upends itself
	There are candles
	Drinks
	All went flying
	Somebody else kicked me
	A woman I think
	In fact a rather ugly unedifying scene all round
	And the bouncers picked me up and threw me out
	Arse up

All we needed was one of those swing door
thingies and it would have been a cowboy film
And there I was lying in this street
Somewhere
Fuck knows where
It smelt of fast food
And I can hear people taking the piss
They keep peering down at me as though I'm some
sort of freak exhibit who's been plonked there for
their amusement
And I think I must go home
I must fucking stop this
I must
Oh Christ I felt tired
Suddenly
It steals over my pathetic drunken heap
Knackeredness in extremis
And as I'm lying there
I think of Mick
On his slab
On his death slab
Dead
Grim-reaped
Not with us any more

HOLLY   And I closed my eyes and tried to imagine what it would be like

HENRY   Not thinking

HOLLY   And I felt sick

HENRY   Not feeling

HOLLY   Really sick
At the thought of

HENRY   Not
Anything

HOLLY   Nothing

(*Silence.* KEV *enters.*)

KEV   I couldn't sleep
      I was tired but I couldn't settle
      And I could hear upstairs
      Moving about
      Laughing
      But eventually they stopped
      And I thought I'll never be able to get up for work tomorrow at this rate
      And it felt
      Quiet
      But I wasn't going to drop off
      You know sometimes it's not going to happen
      So I got up
      And had a bowl of cereal
      Shreddies
      And I stood at the window
      It was something like four o'clock
      And I thought
      You know what they say about four o'clock in the morning
      It's a low ebb apparently
      Nobody was about
      Not even a light on
      And I thought
      And I'm not sure why I did this
      I checked my heartbeat
      At first I couldn't find it
      It's quite difficult if you don't know what you're doing
      But then there it was
      I could feel it
      Definitely
      There it was
      Still going

      (*Lights down. Lights up.*)

HENRY The front door
       Someone was ringing the front door
       This was the following morning now
       I was home
       Somehow
       And I was deeply comatose
       With the emphasis on coma

And someone is holding their finger down on the bell
And I think is this a theme in my life all of a sudden
And with this onslaught of consciousness it all comes flooding back
Mick
Dead
Things to do
Oh fuck
And along with all that I cannot help but register that I am the solitary owner of the mother of all hangovers
Actually the word hangover does it a disservice
It's more a toxic fog in the shape of an evil dwarf that is scraping a blunt screwdriver round the inside of my head
But I stumble out of my pit
And whoever it is they're still intermittently ringing the fucking thing
And I'm thinking
I am thinking
Shut up will you please shut up I am not well I am seriously not well
And also it makes this dreadful farty sound
Like a dying fly amplified fifty fold
But I get to it open it
And
Fuck
It's what's-his-face
Bloke from the pub
Him
Kev
Standing on the doorstep
And the sun is shining
How lovely
And he's standing there
And in his hand
It's the first thing I notice
He's holding a bag of black bin liners

KEV   I, I explained that I'd been waiting at Mick's flat
And I thought that
You know, seeing as it was

It was getting on for eleven by now
Something like that
And that, well, nobody was there
And I thought
Because Henry had said
I thought
He had said he wouldn't mind a hand
He wasn't looking too hot actually
He was squinting very badly and he was still wearing last night's shirt
And no trousers
And I, I said
If he wanted me to come back later that was no problem
I'd taken the rest of the week off work
Not that I told Henry that
So if he did want me to come back later on
No problem
Actually I'd picked up some bin liners as well
Thought we might need them
Extra strength ones
Very good
Always use them for my own purposes
And I was explaining all this
And I couldn't help noticing that Henry wasn't
He wasn't saying much
He was just
He was sort of just squinting at me
It was a lovely day actually
Crisp but sunny
But eventually Henry said

HENRY   Wait there

KEV   And he shut the door and went off

HENRY   Kev
Fucking Dr who's that then
As he's known behind his back
Kev
Mister fucking personality
On the doorstep
What the fu –
And I was not in a good mood

	Understatement I had got a major civil war scenario raging inside my cranium and now here was Kev File under charisma, lack of Going Looking at me as though Bin liners extra strength Oh for fucks sake And I'm banging about thinking all this I am a right miserable bastard sometimes And I, I made myself a coffee And I had a shower Felt marginally better Cut myself shaving Felt marginally worse Had another coffee Had a monumental shit Felt quite a bit better Had another coffee Smoked three fags, thought I might throw up, didn't Felt well enough to walk in a straightish line And went to sort out Mick's flat. With Kev.
Kev	Mick's flat, it's not far from Henry's.
Henry	I think we worked out once that I was nearer to The Bulls Head by forty yards.
Kev	I remember that Max worked it out with one of those wheel measuring things that civil engineers use
Henry	Ah yes the good old days
Kev	Still, it was nice to see a bit of sun
Henry	I was wishing for fucking rain
Kev	Henry didn't give the impression of wanting to chat much

HENRY And then we got there

KEV The downstairs neighbour had the key for some reason

HENRY Mick mansions
As it was known

KEV There was no blood on the stairs or anything
Not that I thought there would be
But
There wasn't

HENRY And we went up the stairs
And there was his door

KEV And the hallway
Henry went in first
The hallway was
Dark
No windows
And there was a distinct
I've always noticed with these old Victorian places
There's always a chill

HENRY And then there was the front room
The door was slightly ajar
And it felt
And I realised

KEV Mick obviously wasn't a man who believed in interior decor

HENRY I hadn't really given this moment much thought beforehand

KEV We both went quiet

HENRY It all looked
As though
Fuck

KEV We just stood there

HENRY	As though he was coming back sometime

(*Silence.*)

KEV	I put the kettle on
HENRY	It was as much as it ever was
KEV	And there was a mug with something in it next to the kettle.
HENRY	There was a huge heap of dog-ends spilling over an ashtray And a copy of *The News of the World*
KEV	And the end of some chips
HENRY	And his telly And a beer mat on the top of it
KEV	There was a bit of washing up
HENRY	Videos A biro He'd obviously been writing what he'd been recording And I thought that was bloody organised of him
KEV	A frying pan, two or three plates A j-cloth that had seen better days
HENRY	*Only Fools and Horses* *The Royle Family* Something I couldn't make out But it was Mick's writing
KEV	An electricity bill Red Still in its envelope In the window sill
HENRY	A plastic bag with an empty packet of fags in

KEV   A champagne cork with 10p jammed in it

HENRY   And all his records
Alphabetical order
Leaning there underneath the window
I know he used to have hundreds
But he'd sold most of them over the years
And there were a few scattered about
Cat Stevens
Miles Davis
The Velvet Underground

KEV   One of the drawers next to the cooker was missing

HENRY   Cat Stevens was on the turntable

KEV   And there was a whiff
Not a bad whiff
But the definite beginnings of something

HENRY   And I thought
Fucking hell

KEV   So I opened the window

HENRY   Fancy Cat Stevens being the last thing you ever listen to

KEV   And I made the tea and took it through to Henry

HENRY   And I thought

KEV   He took it without looking at me

HENRY   He had fuck all didn't he
At the end of the day
He had sweet fanny nothing

(Beat.)

KEV   We decided I'd start in the kitchen
And Henry would do the bedroom

HENRY	And that was a strange day Raking through the oddments and leftovers of one Michael Finnegan
KEV	The kitchen was Well it needed attention paying to it, let's say that The oven was caked And the grill Well I'd say there was at least half an inch
HENRY	Stripping his bed All the newspapers underneath The wardrobe full of clothes The two porn mags from the early nineties I presume they had some sentimental attachment
KEV	Drawers full of stuff Rawlplugs Elastic bands Plastic bags And there was quite a bit of it that was half decent For example, there was a bag of screws unopened So that sort of thing I put to one side for Oxfam
HENRY	Kev made me us a cup of tea every hour or so And after he'd done the kitchen He started on the bathroom
KEV	There was quite a bit of mould
HENRY	That was a very strange thing we were doing that day At the time though
KEV	Basically I threw out everything
HENRY	At the time though You just get on with it
KEV	I was Strange to say this But I was quite enjoying myself That's not the right word

| | But
| | I was

HENRY   And we'd been there a few hours
         Could have been several actually
         I was still in Mick's bedroom
         I'd managed a few bags of rubbish to be got rid of
         But there was stuff like
         Shoeboxes of his scribblings
         And his guitar
         Missing a couple of strings but still
         What was I going to do with it?
         And then
         I was sitting there
         I'd found a copy of *The Mirror* from the day
         Lennon died
         I was going to keep that
         And I heard
         Faintish
         Drifting in from the front room
         No doubt about it
         Cat Stevens
         Drifting down the corridor
         And
         Kev
         Kev was singing along

KEV   I was just giving myself a little break
         After all my hard work

HENRY   Kev was singing along to Cat Stevens
         And I thought
         I thought I wasn't entirely sure if I was happy with this
         That was Mick's last record
         And
         Actually
         Who is this bloke?
         I don't know him.
         Obviously I know him
         But
         Mick always gave him the time of day
         But that was Mick
         He'd talk to anyone

                    Jesus, who did he think he was?
                    He comes in the pub most nights but he says fuck all
                    And here he was
                    Singing along to the last record Mick ever listened to
                    And so I went through to the front room
                    And he was still humming along
                    And he was flicking through Mick's records as well
                    And then
                    He could tell I was in the room
                    He looked up

KEV   I didn't think Henry would mind

HENRY   And I said, quite calm, considered, what are you doing?

KEV   But then I thought
            Oh dear he does

HENRY   And it was as if
            Excuse me, have you heard what I've just said?

KEV   And I felt a bit awkward
            And I, I
            Could feel myself going red

HENRY   And I said it again
            What are you doing?

KEV   I, I didn't know what to say
            So I said
            What do you mean?

HENRY   And I thought
            Who is this idiot
            But I answered his question
            What are you doing playing Mick's records?
            I said
            And he didn't bat an eyelid
            He just
            Nothing

| | And I said it again, extra-slow this time
And still he just |
|-------|---|
| KEV | I felt terrible
I felt
I shouldn't have done that
I shouldn't have put on that record |
| HENRY | And very quietly
He goes |
KEV	I'm sorry.
HENRY	What?
KEV	I'm sorry
HENRY	And he says this in such a way that I think
KEV	I'm sorry
HENRY	He's going to crap himself he's so
KEV	I'm sorry
Honestly I'm really sorry
HENRY	And I think maybe I have over-reacted
But then he says
KEV	I'd better get going
HENRY	And he picks his jacket up off the sofa
And he sort fumbles his way past me
And I say what are you doing
And he says he's off
And I say there's no need for that
He doesn't have to go
But he's adamant
And he says I can keep the bin-bags
And the cleaning stuff he bought as well
And I think
And he's going down the corridor
Stay here oi stay
And then he's out the door

And
The front door goes
And
He's gone
Kev has left the building

(*Beat.*)

And Cat Stevens is still warbling away
And I cut him off mid-something
And I put him back in his sleeve
And
I put all Mick's records back
They're not in good nick
Just looking at a few of them
But I play an old Dylan
Something I haven't heard
Must be nearly twenty years
And I think
It's a long time since I just sat and listened
Especially Dylan
And I listen to that voice and all those words
Sometimes they make sense
And sometimes
It's just Dylan
And it finishes
And
I sit there
I sit there until I notice the hum of the speaker

(*Beat.*)

So I go back to the bedroom
And I notice there's a small pile of books next to the bed
All sorts
I haven't had a look at them yet
And there's a Graham Greene
Old Penguin edition
And
There's a strip of passport photographs
Just the top half
Mick was obviously using it as a bookmark
And

I turn it over
And
It's Holly
A few years back down the line
But it's Holly
There she is
She looks startled in the top one
Like someone's about to run her over
But then in the next
She's smiling
Open
Happy

(*Beat.*)

And the next thing I remember
I'm aware of
Is how dark everything's got
I've been asleep
I'd fallen asleep on Mick's bed
Dragged his duvet over me
But I have no idea what the time is
It's not late late
But I feel
Disorientated
There's a television
Off
Downstairs
Canned laughter
And I get up
Splash my face in the bathroom
I've never seen it looking so sodding clean
And the light bulb is about to die
I feel grim actually
Badly dehydrated
So I go to the kitchen
Get myself a glass of water
I don't switch on the light
There's a street lamp just outside
Everything's tinged orange
And I'm holding on to the sink
Knocking back my second glass
And there are a few cars
Footsteps

Dust to Dust

High heels
And a shout
Night sounds
And it's a bit chilly
Fucking cold actually
And there's that shout again
Off somewhere
Not nearby
It's
And I look out of Mick's kitchen window
The streetlight
A cat
Not a lot happening
And I think I'd better go
Sleep in my own bed
Christ I feel worn out
Hung up
Dried
And just plain
And then there's that shout again
Always sounds the same
Like
A bark maybe
No it's not a dog
It's more like
And there it is again
It's a short snap of sound
Is it from inside the house?
That's what I'm thinking
And I go to the corridor
Try to find the light switch
Fuck knows where it is
By the door somewhere
So I open door on to the landing to see where it is
And
As I find it
There's something
I notice something
Down the stairs
And
I know what it is but I don't
I step out
And there
Standing

One step from the bottom
With his back to me
Was Mick
And I'm here and he's there
It's Mick
Un-fucking mistakable
Just
Standing there
And he walks down the hall
Still with his back to me
But it's him
The jeans
His hair
The bald patch coming through at the back
And
His walk
It's him
And he goes he walks
Down the hallway
Into shadow
The dark
It's
Mick
He was there
As though I could
He was there
I wait
I breathe
I wait
I can still hear canned laughter
Shit
Shit
I switched on every light in his flat
I must go home
Yes
I thought that
I'll go home
And I was pacing up and down
He was there
I saw him
Mick
Mick
I couldn't stay still
Shit

I sat on his bed
I got up
Into the kitchen
I looked in the cupboards see if there was any booze secreted anywhere
Ah fuck it
And then
I'm thinking I must go home
This is too bizarre
This is too
And then
Cross my heart and hope to die
No I didn't say that
And then
The phone starts ringing
It's partly hidden
Behind the telly
But it starts ringing
And I stop
It rings four times
I watch it ring
And then
Oh Christ
The answer machine
Mick's voice
There it was
In the room
It's a crappy machine and the tape is playing a bit slow
But there it was
It was short
No nonsense
He sounded slightly embarrassed
But it was Mick
And whoever it was
On the other end
They didn't leave a message
They hung up
And then
Just a few seconds later
The phone rang again
And I thought
I picked it up on the fourth ring
Hello?

HOLLY	And there was a voice A real voice
HENRY	Hello?
HOLLY	Henry Shit
HENRY	Hello? Who is this?
HOLLY	I didn't say anything
HENRY	Look hello Come on what's going on here?
HOLLY	There was no way I was going to say anything
HENRY	Who is this?

(HOLLY *makes a slight noise.*)

HENRY	Who is that?
HOLLY	What are you doing there?
HENRY	Holly?
HOLLY	Oh no
HENRY	Holly? What on Earth
HOLLY	What was he doing there?
HENRY	Holly?
HOLLY	I didn't think anybody would be there
HENRY	Holly? Answer me? Holly? Oh for crying out loud will you just And then I realised

HOLLY	I'd done nothing all day I'd dozed a lot I wasn't up to much to be honest I watched telly Read magazines Anything to make me think of something else Or not think As the case may be
HENRY	I realised why Holly was calling
HOLLY	I just wanted to hear his voice That was all

(*Beat.*)

HOLLY	It was an off-chance I didn't even know if he had an answer machine

(*Silence.*)

HENRY	And then out of this silence
HOLLY	This awkwardness
HENRY	Stranger things have happened but
HOLLY	We started talking
HENRY	I think we both felt
HOLLY	We needed it
HENRY	Not that either of us would ever
HOLLY	No no no Jesus no
HENRY	We agreed to meet up the next day
HOLLY	There was still a lot to organise
HENRY	I didn't tell her about I thought

	I'll tell her tomorrow
HOLLY	And then we hung up
HENRY	And I went home Out of the flat And down the stairs

(*Beat.*)

	As far as I could tell He wasn't about
HOLLY	Henry told me the next day About Mick I was intrigued I didn't believe him That goes without saying To be honest I don't think Henry even believed himself
HENRY	You know In the cold light of day Etcetera etcetera
HOLLY	And there was stuff to do
HENRY	Money stuff
HOLLY	Funeral stuff
HENRY	Legal stuff
HOLLY	Stuff
HENRY	The banality of death
HOLLY	It's a wonderful thing when you need it
HENRY	And we ended up at Mick's flat
HOLLY	There were a few things I thought I might like
HENRY	I never mentioned the photographs

HOLLY   You know just something
         Nothing much

HENRY   We talked about the music for the funeral

HOLLY   We played a few things

HENRY   And after that

HOLLY   We settled on The Stones

HENRY   It was beginning to get dark

HOLLY   Neither of us

HENRY   Mentioned the fact

HOLLY   But

HENRY   We kept one ear

         (*They react slightly.*)

HOLLY   Was, that?

HENRY   I think, er

HOLLY   Outside?

HENRY   No, no, just

         (*Still.*)

HOLLY   That was a knock

HENRY   Do you think?

HOLLY   I'm sure, something

HENRY   Are you sure, I, I, could have sworn

HOLLY   Definitely

HENRY   Holly

HOLLY   And I was down the corridor

HENRY   Honestly Holly I think it was just

HOLLY   And out on to the landing

HENRY   And there standing

HOLLY   At the top of the stairs
         Was

         (KEV *appears*.)

HENRY   Kev

KEV   I thought you might be hungry

HENRY   With a family-size pizza

HOLLY   And some beer

KEV   I'd seen the light on
         I'd sort of been keeping an eye out actually
         Just wandered past every now and then
         Henry he, he didn't say anything about the
         You know the
         The incident with the record
         And Holly she
         She didn't seem to
         She didn't say anything either

HOLLY   The pizza was very welcome

KEV   I heard about Mick
         The night before
         Henry seemed to be treating it as a bit of a joke
         But as he was retelling it
         The hairs
         On the back of my neck

HENRY   I'm not normally a lager man

KEV	And so we sat in Mick's flat
HENRY	But in the circumstances
KEV	And we thought about Mick
HENRY	I made an exception
KEV	And we talked about Mick
HOLLY	Our wedding day And the piss-up, sorry, the reception afterwards Henry's pitiful pitiful speech
HENRY	I lost my notes
HOLLY	And Mick's uncle's dandruff
HENRY	He's dead now Lung cancer
HOLLY	And the bridesmaids Carol the Goth
HENRY	Ah yes Carol
HOLLY	Her black lipstick
HENRY	Hey whatever happened to Carol?
HOLLY	She lives in Surrey
HENRY	Apparently she manages a Little Chef
KEV	And the honeymoon
HOLLY	Scotland Mick's motorbike
HENRY	I always thought you and leather were very well suited Holly
HOLLY	Did you?

HENRY	I suppose you think that's sexist
HOLLY	How he wanted to go and live up there
HENRY	Mick's dream
HOLLY	Apparently he still went on about it every now and then
HENRY	Not so much recently
KEV	It was the first I'd ever heard of it
HOLLY	Scotland this Scotland that I mean what would you do all day?
HENRY	Mick's dream on as I called it
HOLLY	Mick's dream on Very apt
KEV	I thought it sounded quite a good idea personally
HENRY	Mick's dream on
HOLLY	Like his music
KEV	The fishing would have been really good
HOLLY	Eh?
KEV	I'm just saying The fishing, up there, would have been, you know Really good
	(*Beat.*)
HOLLY	And we talked about all the bands he'd been in over the years
HENRY	Calamity Jane
HOLLY	Oh my God they were dreadful

HENRY	The drummer wanted them to dress up as cowboys
HOLLY	Oh yes mister all we need is a gimmick
HENRY	The Shift
HOLLY	The Boat People
HENRY	Peter Out and The Faders
HOLLY	I never saw them
HENRY	Yes they disappeared without a trace
HOLLY	Thing
HENRY	Eh?
HOLLY	Thing Thing !?
HENRY	Oh yes how could I forget The heavy metal years
HOLLY	What a name? Thing
HENRY	They were always going to play Glastonbury
HOLLY	Ah yes
KEV	They were going to play Glastonbury?
HENRY	But somehow it never happened
HOLLY	No It never happened
HENRY	I always fancied dropping acid at Glastonbury
KEV	Free Beer
HOLLY	Eh?
KEV	Free Beer

HENRY   Are you alright Kev?

KEV   I remember Mick saying he wanted to be in a band called Free Beer
You know because
He always thought it would look good on a poster

HOLLY   That's the thing with Mick

HENRY   Would look good on a poster
I'll give him that

HOLLY   Everything comes back to drink in the end

(*Beat.*)

HENRY   It was actually quite late by then

HOLLY   All the beer had gone

KEV   I would have got some more but all the offie's would have been shut

(*Beat.*)

KEV   And we sat there for a bit

HENRY   And we
I can't remember what we did exactly

HOLLY   I think we were

KEV   Nobody said anything for quite sometime

HOLLY   Half-hoping maybe

KEV   I wouldn't want to say what anyone else was thinking but

HENRY   It started raining

HOLLY   Lightly

KEV   But apart from that

HENRY   There was nobody about

HOLLY   No

HENRY   Nobody

         (*Silence.*)

KEV   And Henry and Holly both fell asleep
         We had the fire up high
         Henry said it wasn't as though they were going to get Mick for the bill now were they
         And I drifted on and off
         It wasn't very comfortable to be honest
         And the sun started coming up
         And I thought I'll get off
         A few things to do all that
         I made them both a cup of tea and left it next to them
         It was dead early
         You could tell there had been a bit of rain
         There were a few milk-floats
         They make a funny sound don't they?
         And I had a few hours' kip
         Spruced myself up
         And got a forty-six from outside the library
         It's always quite a journey
         At least
         Just over an hour
         I'm often the only person who stays on all the way
         And then it comes to the end
         A little parade of shops
         I always get a pasty from the Sayers there
         And then I walk it
         And that must be
         Another good ten minutes
         I tell you
         I wouldn't fancy getting a taxi all the way up there

HOLLY   I gave them a ring
         And they said fine
         Two o'clock

That afternoon
Just turn up
And I thought shall I dress up?
But then I thought
Holly that is ridiculous

HENRY
Call me Alan
That's what he kept saying on the phone
Call me Alan
Just call me Alan
I think it was one of the first times he'd done this sort of thing
And we arranged to meet up
He wanted to come to mine
But I thought that wouldn't be
We don't want that
I'd feel under pressure to tidy up
So we met at his
Just a chat
Just a chat
He kept saying that as well

KEV
Maureen is always in the hallway
She must be there all day asking people who they're looking for
Apparently she used to run a sweet shop
The lounge was quite busy
I think they'd been playing records
I asked Maureen if they'd been playing records
But she was more interested in giving me directions
You take a right
Past the dining room and that smell you always get
And there's a little ramp
And then there's quite a long corridor
And up at the top there's a fishtank
I always stop and have a look in
Quite a big thing it is
All sorts of fish
I don't know any of the breeds but
Very impressive
And then it's not far
There's a few rooms on the left

The laundry room as well
And there she is
In her chair
The telly's on
The telly's always on
She used to look out of the window quite a bit
But she doesn't do that any more
'Hello Mum'
I say

HOLLY   The funeral place
Shop
Whatever it is
I must have walked past it
Hundreds of times
And I never thought about
Why should you?
It's a family firm
There was a young girl at the desk
She called through
And Mr Havelock emerged
He remembered me from the other day
When we'd been in choosing the coffin
Fancy
Everyday
Death
And he said
That if I wanted to go through
I could

HENRY   Alan was a man for whom the Christmas jumper
was invented
He was
I suppose if you are going to set yourself up as a
lay preacher it's a reasonable quality to possess
He was on the keen side
And I was right
It was only his third funeral
He told me that within a few minutes
And I was thinking
Too much information
He was very good at eye contact
And the flat was
Inoffensive to the point of offensive

If you know what I mean
And we chatted
Dissected the life of our dearly departed
Amazingly he wasn't that sniffy re Mick's general
lifestyle and lack nay complete and total disregard
for any form of spirituality
Actually he was alright
For a poor man's vicar he was alright

KEV Mum has stopped talking pretty much
I mean, only recently has she
Stopped all together
She still smiles occasionally but she doesn't know
who I am
There was a time when she thought I was Dad
She was gripping on to her beaker thing
Apparently it could still be years
You know
Until
A neighbour was telling me about her Grandad
There was an afternoon chat show thing on
Whatshisname was singing
That Irish fellar
All the women fancy him
And I sat there
And we still chat
Well, I do
And I told Mum about Mick
And Henry
And Holly
And about everything that had been going on
I left out a few details but covered most of it
And I held her hand
Something else was on now
Something to do with flower arranging

HOLLY I don't know what I expected
I wasn't entirely sure if it was him at first
But
There he was
He was wearing his only suit
And a clean pair of undies
I knew that because Henry had taken them down
the other day

And yes it was the suit he got married in
And yea knowing Mick it was probably the
underpants as well
He looked
The lighting wasn't great
It tended towards the
Atmospheric
He looked
Stupid
Odd
No weird
Not Mick
He was wearing make-up for a start
Lipstick and
Too much rouge mate
That's what I thought
And once I was there
I mean
I hadn't told anybody I was doing this
I think I wanted something, an experience
But once I was there
As seems to be a common thread in my life
I thought
Why on earth have I done this?

HENRY
And I'd finished the coffee
Possibly the blandest I've ever tasted
And I'd agreed to do the, the speech
The er, what's it called
Anyway, that
I thought maybe I could have carried the coffin
but apparently that wasn't going to be necessary
So I was just about to depart
When he says
Alan
He says
Would you mind if we said a small prayer for
Mick?

KEV
And a bit later on
The nurses brought in some tea
They wondered why I was there
You know
If I was on holiday

So I told them about Mick
And Mum fell asleep
And I thought
She looked as though she might disappear
down the side of the armchair
And I thought
Getting old
Why would anyone want to get old?
And I thought
Mick
He won't be getting old
Like Princess Diana

HOLLY   He's dead
Whatever that means
He's dead
And he's not coming back

HENRY   And we sat in this stranger's kitchen
Alan shut his eyes and we
And I'm not greatly proud of this
But we held hands
And I thought
Actually if I'm honest I thought
I wish I was seeing Mick that night because this
was a fuck of a good story
And Alan said his prayer
His few words
What they were
Can't remember
But basically he wished all the best for Mick's
soul
Some hope

KEV   And I gave Mum a little kiss
And I walked back down the corridor
Past the fish tank
Past all the other rooms
And all the old people sitting there
Watching telly
Waiting

(*Change.*)

HOLLY	And then Life It carried on As it tends to
HENRY	Mick's finances were a nightmare But that's another story
KEV	I phoned up work Arranged another couple of days
HOLLY	Those few days before a funeral
HENRY	You seem to be hanging about a lot
HOLLY	I bought a dress
HENRY	I kept making notes Trying to put together my thoughts about what I was going to say about the old bastard
HOLLY	And then it's the morning of
KEV	I'd set my alarm clock Although to be honest I was already awake when it went off
HOLLY	The weather wasn't up to much
HENRY	Sort of grey with a hint of grey
KEV	And the forecast didn't give much cause for hope
HOLLY	Oh well
HENRY	Max turned up early It was a midday kick-off Strange seeing people wearing jackets and ties all of a sudden And he He had a few cans secreted about his person And he said In that way he does Care to join me

HOLLY   A few of us were going to follow the coffin
And we'd arranged to meet at Henry's beforehand

KEV   I went and got Dad's car
It's one of those old Austin Princesses
You know so I could follow behind
We keep it in a garage near the Asda
We've just never got round to selling it
It didn't sound great when I first turned it on
So I had a quick look under the bonnet
And then the fellar opposite
He needed a shove
And after I'd done that
Time was a bit short
So I thought
I don't want to be late
And I put me foot down
And
The traffic wasn't great
And
I got there at the same time as the coffin

HENRY   Always a salutary moment

HOLLY   Henry finished his drink

HENRY   I could tell she wasn't too happy
But give the girl her due
She didn't say anything

KEV   And we all set off
I was at the back

HOLLY   Nobody said much

HENRY   And I was thinking
Maybe I should have had a spot of breakfast

KEV   And I remembered the last time I was doing this

HOLLY   There was a supermarket
As busy as ever

KEV	With Dad
HENRY	We went past a school
HOLLY	There was a group of boys running around like a bunch of headless chickens
HENRY	And then we turned off
HOLLY	And worked our way up
HENRY	And there it was
KEV	And we parked up
HENRY	Crematoriums Why do they all look like village halls trying to be trendy?
KEV	And there was a group of people Off to the left Looking at the flowers They'd obviously only just finished
HOLLY	And we assembled Formed an orderly queue
HENRY	There were quite a few faces Alan appeared, touched flesh And I couldn't help thinking So that's who buys beige suits then
HOLLY	None of my family I thought maybe But it would appear not
KEV	And we got the nod And we started filing in
HENRY	And I thought I could do with a piss It wasn't a big thought But it did skip through my head

HOLLY	The coffin had been placed on what looked like a It looked like a huge formica table
KEV	Somebody seemed to be playing the organ And I thought that's strange because And I realised it was a tape
HENRY	And I'm not sure but I think was there a gents back there In the foyer
HOLLY	Henry and myself were seated at the front
KEV	I was a few rows back
HENRY	I'd only be gone a minute or so
HOLLY	And then it started
KEV	They don't hang about at these places
HENRY	And Alan was fumbling and farting away at the front Leaning on his lectern He kept throwing me the odd glance I checked my jacket pocket The notes for Mick's eulogy That's what it's called by the way And Oh fuck I could actually do with a piss Let nature do its course And somehow I thought I could feel my bladder actually pushing its way And I thought Don't be a fucking idiot Henry It was only two cans of Guinness And I'm sure there was a lav back there And I notice As I'm thinking all this And Alan is still monotoning on I notice

My notes
Mick's eulogy
I've got them clasped in my hand
I've scrunched them all up
And I try and unscrunch them
And
My palms
They're wet
And
I really should have a piss
I don't want to be thinking about this when
And these notes
Oh Jesus
They're a mess
I can't understand a word of them looking at them
They just seem like so much bullshit
They look like some fucking obscure hieroglyphics
Shit
I have got to go and have a piss
I really must
I really actually need
And Alan is doing something
He's looking at me
Any minute now
He's going to say
Oh fuck me
What a pantomime
And I think
One last time
I have got to go and have a piss

KEV   And Henry gets up

HOLLY   At first I think
But then I realise
He's actually

KEV   He walks out

HOLLY   Alan stops
And we all turn and watch as

KEV   He walks straight out the door
Through the foyer

	And outside
HOLLY	And then he goes round the corner Out of sight
KEV	He disappears
HOLLY	And
KEV	Everyone looks at everyone else
HOLLY	Alan sort of coughs
KEV	He's obviously like the rest of us thinking
HOLLY	What the fuck is going on?
KEV	Without the fuck obviously
HOLLY	And we sit there And Alan tries to start again And Henry He doesn't seem to be
KEV	He's been gone a few minutes now
HOLLY	And then Kev gets up and
KEV	I slip out to try and see what's what And I don't see him at first But there he is He's standing by a flowerbed There are quite a few of those remembrance plaques dotted amongst it And I thought There's steam coming off some of those plants And Henry was just Standing there He was breathing funny And he didn't look up So I put my hand on his shoulder Just

You know
Just to let him know I was there

(*Beat.*)

HOLLY Alan cut it short

KEV I think the people at the crematorium
Not that I have anything to back this up
But I think they were quite pleased
You know because they were running a bit late

HENRY And we stood in the foyer
And watched
The very end

HOLLY There was a whirr

HENRY A slight shudder

KEV And the coffin it

HOLLY It disappeared

KEV I always thought a curtain came across

HENRY No it just sort of

HOLLY Descended into the

KEV I don't like to think about that bit

HENRY And even The Stones sounded

HOLLY Not quite right

KEV And that was it

HOLLY We stood around for a bit

HENRY Nobody mentioned my
My little faux pas

HOLLY The weather was still

	A sort of nothing
KEV	It started drizzling
HENRY	We'd booked a buffet back at The Bulls Head
KEV	Sandwiches Quiche Not a bad little spread
HOLLY	I tried to chat to Mick's brother but he's not very He's a strange man I just gave up in the end
KEV	And there was a group of blokes Shouting at the cricket
HENRY	Mick hated cricket
HOLLY	And they'd obviously kept all the sandwiches in the freezer overnight And had just taken them out
HENRY	And even after quite a few pints I didn't feel very much Just a sort of dull headache
KEV	Everyone seemed Very polite
HOLLY	The landlord came round And I could tell he was a bit embarrassed
HENRY	He said that he'd been on to the brewery And they'd said Basically That they weren't too keen on the idea that Mick's ashes would live behind the bar Something to do with Health and Safety regs So basically No can do And I thought Fucking typical

KEV	Henry looked a bit crestfallen
HOLLY	People started drifting off
KEV	It was quite a sedate affair Considering
HENRY	The coleslaw remained undisturbed
KEV	We lost the cricket
HOLLY	And there was just a few of us left

(*Beat.*)

HOLLY Henry
I'll
I'll see you

KEV And that was it
No big anything
We all just got off early
That was it
We went home

(*Beat.*)

And
I went back to work
A few people asked you know
What had I been doing, how was the funeral
But they were just making conversation
That way people do
And
Everything was
Everything had just gone back to being
Normal

(*Beat.*)

And
I was sitting there
At my desk
Only two days after the funeral this was

And someone was talking about last night's telly
And I thought
I'd been thinking about the do in The Bulls Head
And I thought
Maybe, you know, why not
It was just a thought, an idea

(*Beat.*)

So I went to see Henry
And he
He looked terrible actually
Said he'd had a spot of flu
And I said it's probably this Spanish one
And I told him what I'd been thinking about
And he listened
And he said
Well he didn't say much actually
He just put his jacket on
And we headed off to the crematorium
And we picked up Mick
The ashes
You might not know this
But you don't actually get the ashes on the actual day
You have to wait a bit
Because apparently
They have to cool down
And I paid for a nice little urn
And then after we'd done that
We called round for Holly
And
She was in
And we explained
She looked a bit mystified at first
But then she said give her a minute
And she got her handbag and a few things
And we set off
In my Dad's Austin Princess
We set off
We headed up towards the M62
We got a few looks
You don't see many of them on the roads these days

But it wasn't too busy
And we were chatting
Catching up
You know like
Like people who know a bit about each other
And then the M6
That was quite a bit busier
Quite a few lorries
And I thought I'm not going to overdo it
I'll just keep to the inside lane
And there was a discussion on the radio
About the Millennium Dome and what they're
going do with it
And Henry ranted on for a bit
I didn't say anything because the only person I
know who went said she quite enjoyed it
And before you know it
We were up near Carlisle
We stopped at a service station
Holly bought a big bar of chocolate
And I noticed
The women behind the tills
They all had this accent
Nothing weird
It was just different
That's it all was
Different
And also I noticed
We were still in England
But I noticed there seemed to be more
Space
And then there was the sign saying Scotland
We crossed the border
And I remembered a time from when I was a kid
And my dad telling me why we'd never been to
Scotland was because we needed a passport
And I believed him
And we had a look at the map
Very straightforward
M74 all the way to Glasgow
You go past Lockerbie
And we're still talking and everything
And then

To be honest I didn't realise you could do it so
quickly
We're coming into Glasgow
Henry said something about how all they do up
here is eat lard and have fights
But actually it looked alright
I liked the look of it and the buildings and
We almost got lost at one point
But we figured it out
And then
Not far out of Glasgow
There's Loch Lomond
Fantastic
You turn a corner and there it is
And Holly told us a story about her and Mick
They were camping nearby
And a rattlesnake
You can get them up here apparently
But we didn't stop
Although I was thinking maybe I should have
brought my camera
And Henry said we'll find somewhere to stay in a
bit
So after a bit
We stopped at a pub
For a bite to eat
Henry asks if they do deep fried mars bars
They're not too amused
But they've actually got haggis on the menu
And I gave it a try
Not half bad at all
And Holly asked if they've got any rooms
But they've only got the one family room
That we could all fit into if we wanted to
So
We decide to carry on
Henry reckons we'll find somewhere in Fort
William
And so we kept going
We're motoring along
And Henry and Holly
They nod off
They'd both had a couple of drinks back at the
pub

And after a bit we hit Fort William
And they were still asleep
And I was thinking
I'll just keep on for a few more miles
You know because the more miles we get under
our belt tonight the better
And you notice
There's quite a few mountains
And those signs about falling rocks
And it was dark now as well
And you have to cut across
It is the most direct way believe it or not
You have to do a sort of zig-zag
Across Scotland
You follow Loch Ness for a bit
I couldn't see it but I knew it was there
And there's the odd pub
But I was thinking I'll just wait until one of them
wakes up
We'll make a decision then
And I kept going
And then you take a turning a bit before Inverness
Henry was snoring
And Holly woke up at one point and said
'Where are we?'
And then she fell straight back to sleep
And then
I was doing very well
And then
Obviously I'm compressing things quite a bit here
There's Ullapool
And even though it was dark
You could see it from way off
Because all the buildings they're white
And the moon was out
Not quite full but
It was sitting there in the sky
It was quite a moment
And I thought
I'll come back here one day
I'll come back here and do some fishing
But I kept on going
And the car is holding up really well

And I think of Dad and how I wish I knew what he
knew about engines
And I have a quick peek at the map and there's
still a bit of a way
And I think
This is the north isn't it
This is the real north
You think of Scotland and you think
Glasgow
Edinburgh
But this
This is somewhere else
And it's now
It's late
I'm normally well tucked up by now
But I kept on going
And there's the occasional car going the other
way
But nobody overtakes me
It feels like it's just me
It's just us
And for a moment I think
It feels like we're the only people on the planet
Heading along this road
With the car lights and everything out there
And I stop for a pee
I have a pee in the middle of nowhere
And they're still asleep
Holly had said she'd been sleeping really badly
And I'm getting that tiredness you get
You know when you haven't been to bed
And for a moment I think
But I'm not giving up now
And I get back in
And I keep going
I'm keeping going
To be honest I'm not sure what's got into me
And the roads aren't great
I've seen better
And Henry
Well he woke up about now
And he sort of blinks
And he just sits there for a bit
I think he's a bit confused as to what's happening

And he woke up Holly
And she doesn't say anything
She just laughs
She laughs one of the maddest laughs I've ever heard
And we are pushing along now
And there's the sun
It starts creeping up
And Henry
He just kept shaking his head
And muttering
Fuck me fuck me
And something about me being a madman
And you can see the landscape now
All the trees bent by the wind
And Holly was looking at the map
And she said keep going
She'd stopped the laughing by now
And I kept going
I just kept on going
And then we reached a place called Durness
And there it is
The edge of Scotland
The end of Britain
The Atlantic Ocean
And it's really
Believe me there's not a lot up there
And Holly says keep going
And I kept going
I kept on going
And then she says take a left
And we bump down this road
And she says ok ok this'll do
And I pull up
And we stop
And I turn the engine off
And

(*Silence.*)

HOLLY   We listen

HENRY   We listen to the sound of sweet bugger nothing

HOLLY	And eventually Henry says something about This being as good a time as any
KEV	And we get out And we walk through what was a caravan park by the look of it
HOLLY	It was
HENRY	And we make our way down some steps Bit of a bloody deathtrap But we manage
KEV	And then we're standing on a beach
HOLLY	It seems huge
HENRY	Nobody else for miles
KEV	There's just us
HOLLY	And up there I can see it The last few bricks of something
HENRY	And I thought What the fuck would you do up here all day?
KEV	And Holly had got the urn
HOLLY	I couldn't figure it out at first It's not something you do every day There's a little mechanism And then
HENRY	There he was
KEV	It sort of spluttered at first But then there was a nice even flow
HOLLY	And I passed him round
KEV	We all had a go

HENRY	There was quite a bit of him to be got rid of
KEV	There was a bit of a breeze
HOLLY	And I think it's probably not him
HENRY	But
KEV	It is
HOLLY	It was Mick
HENRY	And I thought Fuck Life
KEV	And I think we all felt it You know That maybe we should do something
HENRY	Say a few words Mark the moment
HOLLY	But somehow it seemed
KEV	And all I could think of was For he's a jolly good fellow
HOLLY	Unnecessary
KEV	So I kept schtuum
HENRY	Let the silence do it all
	(*Silence.*)
HOLLY	Goodbye Mick
	(*Silence.*)
HENRY	And then he was all gone
KEV	And I remember thinking Bloody hell

	I'm knackered
HOLLY	And as we stood there
The three of us
And
I remember this
It was just a small tiny thing
As we stood there
The sun was dead bright
But it wasn't warm
It was
There was a lot of weather going on
The sky was
Everything seemed to be
Sun
Cloud
Shapes
Everything seemed really
Sharp
And there stretched out in front of us
On the sand
Were our shadows
There
The three misfits
Slightly longer and thinner than the real thing
But they we were
Imprinted on the earth
And then
It was only for a moment
Literally
Something happened
A cloud must have
Because they disappeared
The shadows
They vanished
One minute we were
There
And then the next
And I thought
I thought

(*Music. 'The Wind' by Cat Stevens.*)

HENRY   Does anyone fancy a drink?

HOLLY   Not half

(An image of their three shadows as the lights fade. The end.)